HOBSONS FU...
& A...

GET COOKIN'!

Start Nibblin'

The Main Event

Room for a Pud?

Where to buy Hobsons - back page

First published in Great Britain in 2012

By Hobsons Brewery & Co Ltd, Newhouse Farm, Tenbury Road, Cleobury Mortimer, DY14 8RD.

www.hobsons-brewery.co.uk

ISBN: 978-0-9573716-0-6

A CIP catalogue record for this book is available from the British Library.

While all reasonable care has been taken during the preparation of this book, neither the publisher, nor contributors can accept responsibility for any consequences arising from the use thereof or from the information contained therein.

Home Economist: Lesley Mackley, Ludlow, Shropshire

Photography: Andy Richardson, Shrewsbury, Shropshire

Design: The M Partnership, Lindridge, Worcestershire

Printed and Bound: Orphans Press Ltd, Leominster, Herefordshire

HOBSONS REAL ALES

Try these finest ales with your funkie foods.

Best Bitter
3.8%

A pale brown to amber medium bodied beer has a strong hop character. It's a bitter but with unconventional warm tones of malt that linger on the palate, the complex malty flavours give richness, balanced by the clean hoppy finish. Draught only.

This full-flavoured golden ale has a big voice, a hint of sweetness which is complemented by subtle hop flavours leading to a dry finish. CAMRA Champion Beer of Britain, Bronze Award - Golden Ales 2012.

Town Crier
4.5%

Twisted Spire
3.6%

A unique beer with all round appeal, with a sweet floral aroma, the initial fizz and sweetness gives way to a refreshing burst of hop flavour which lingers through to a crisp dry finish.

CAMRA Champion Beer of Britain 2007, Hobsons Mild has a smooth character and taste notes of chocolate malt which give this beer plenty of coffee flavour and chocolate aroma that belies its strength. Draught only.

Mild
3.2%

Old Henry
5.2%

CAMRA regional 2011 champion brew has complex malty flavours giving a richness that is balanced by a clean hoppy finish. A beer with plenty of character and a good long finish.

A subtle combination of vanilla, treacle and roast malt gives an initial rich sweetness leading to a velvety chocolate finish. It looks stunning in the glass with a tight creamy head.

Postman's Knock
4.8%

Manor Ale
4.2%

With aromas that reflect fresh malted grain and citrus hops, Manor Ale is a crisp refreshing amber bitter with biscuit overtones.

HOBSONS
BREWERY

Hobsons Brewery was born in 1993 with a passion for producing the finest real ales.

Nestled in the heart of Cleobury Mortimer in Shropshire, the Davis family started brewing from a converted sawmill; combining traditional craftsmanship, the finest ingredients and a spirit of fun.

The name Hobsons was born of an amateur dramatics production of "Hobsons Choice" and we adopted Henry for our brand; a character who evoked all that's best in British brewing. Today, his hat - the Coke (pronounced 'cook') remains our trademark, a legacy of no-nonsense quality.

Hobsons Brewery is dedicated to producing beers that use locally-sourced ingredients. Our hop grower, Geoff Thompson, is just down the road and our network of barley growers are all within 30 miles of the brewery. This philosophy has helped us to set the flavours of our casks and bottles apart from the competition. It has also played a crucial part in gaining industry recognition in the form of prestigious awards; such as **CAMRA Champion Beer of Britain 2007 - Hobsons Mild.**

Twisted Spire
3.6
HOBSONS
VIBRANT BLOND BEER

One thing that we take quite seriously is the use of ecologically responsible and sustainable technologies - you can read more about this at the end of the book.

More than anything else, Hobsons is a brewery, a sociable family and a passionate business with a desire to produce distinct, high quality, real ales.

Our commitment to supporting local communities goes beyond the sourcing of ingredients; we get behind our region, its people and its resources. This ethos led to Hobsons sponsoring a rowing boat, setting up a pub cricket league, saving hedgehogs with a limited edition "Old Prickly" charity beer, sponsoring Europe's only inland sea shanty singers and working in partnership with local publicans, . . to name but a few.

EASI CHEESY ALE PUFFS

Louise Taylor - Student, Birmingham University College

INGREDIENTS

Makes 12

65g plain flour

50g butter

150 ml Hobsons Twisted Spire

2 eggs, lightly beaten

1 tsp mustard powder

Freshly ground black pepper

75g mature Cheddar cheese, grated

PREPARATION

1 Preheat the oven to 200C/Gas 6. Line a baking sheet with baking parchment. Sift the flour onto a plate.

2 Place the butter and Hobsons Twisted Spire in a saucepan and heat gently until the butter melts, then bring to the boil. Remove the pan from the heat and tip in the flour, beating vigorously. Return the pan to the heat and continue beating until the mixture is smooth and forms a ball in the centre of the pan. Take care not to overbeat. Remove from the heat and tip the mixture into a large bowl then leave to cool for a few minutes.

3 Gradually add the beaten eggs, using an electric mixer to add air to the mixture. Continue beating until a sheen appears. Stir in the mustard powder, pepper and cheese and mix well.

4 Using a dessert spoon, place golf ball sized mounds of the mixture on the lined baking sheet. Bake in the oven for 15 minutes until risen and golden brown. Serve warm.

CRYIN' OUT FOR CAJUN TROUT

David Gurr Gearing - The Queens, Ludlow

Town Crier

4⅕%

HOBSONS
CRISP GOLDEN ALE

INGREDIENTS

Serves 4

4 tbsp flour

Salt and freshly ground black pepper

4 skinless trout fillets, halved lengthways and cut into goujons

125g dessicated coconut

Oil for deep frying

Chilli crème fraîche or mayonnaise, to serve

For the batter

125g self-raising flour

1 tsp Cajun spice

300 ml Hobsons Town Crier

1 egg, beaten

1 tsp white wine vinegar

PREPARATION

1 To make the batter, place the flour, Cajun spice, Hobsons Town Crier, egg and vinegar in a bowl and whisk to make a smooth batter, the consistency of double cream.

2 In a deep fat fryer, heat the oil to 175C. In a shallow dish, mix together the flour, salt and pepper. Spread the dessicated coconut in a shallow dish. Dip the trout goujons, a few at a time, into the seasoned flour and then into the batter to coat thoroughly. Roll the battered fish in the coconut then fry, in batches, in the hot oil until golden brown and rising in the fryer.

3 Drain the battered fish on kitchen paper and keep warm while frying the remainder. Serve with crème fraîche or mayonnaise which has been seasoned with a little chilli sauce.

DRINK THE REST

DARK ALE & WALNUT LOAF

Peter Cook - Price & Sons Bakery, Ludlow

Old Henry

5.2%

HOBSONS
RICH AUBURN ALE

INGREDIENTS

Makes 1 large loaf

10g fresh yeast

230 ml Hobsons Old Henry

200g strong white bread flour

200g malted flour such as Bacheldre Mill's Organic Stoneground Strong Malted Blend

1 tsp salt

2 tbsp vegetable oil

100g broken walnuts

PREPARATION

1 In a bowl, blend the yeast with a small amount of the Hobsons Old Henry. Leave for 10 minutes.

2 Place the flours and salt in a large bowl and add the yeast mixture. Stir in the oil and remaining Hobsons Old Henry. Mix to a soft dough, adding a little more beer if necessary, then turn out onto a floured board and knead 10 times. Leave for 10 minutes.

3 Knead again for 1 minute and leave for a further 10 minutes. Repeat the 'knead and leave' process about 4 times, letting time do the work.

4 Cover the bowl and leave in a warm place for 30 minutes.

5 Turn out the dough onto a floured surface and knead lightly and briefly to 'knock back'. Shape into a round then place on a floured baking tray and leave to prove until 50% bigger.

6 Preheat the oven to 200C/Gas 6. With a sharp knife, cut a deep cross in the top of the loaf. Bake in the oven for 30 minutes until golden brown.

Baker's tip: If using a mixer to make the dough, place the yeast mixture and all the remaining ingredients in a mixer with a dough hook attached. Mix to a soft dough and knead for 5 minutes, then continue from step 4.

DRINK THE REST

POSTMAN'S KNOCK RAREBIT

Will Holland - La Bécasse, Ludlow

INGREDIENTS

Serves 4

500 ml Hobsons Postman's Knock

40g unsalted butter

50g plain flour

125 ml milk

130g Snowdonia Black Bomber cheese, finely grated

45g Gruyère cheese, finely grated

1 tbsp Dijon mustard

1½ tsp Worcester sauce

1 shake Tabasco sauce

1 pinch cayenne pepper

1 pinch grated nutmeg

1 pinch paprika

Salt and freshly ground black pepper, to taste

8 slices sourdough bread

PREPARATION

1 Place the Hobsons Postman's Knock in a saucepan, bring to the boil and simmer until reduced to 125 ml. Set aside.

2 Place the butter in a saucepan and melt over a medium heat. Add the flour and cook, stirring continuously, for one minute. Gradually stir in the milk and reduced beer. Continue to cook, stirring, until boiling, then remove from the heat. Add the grated cheeses and stir until melted. Stir in the mustard, Worcester sauce, Tabasco sauce, cayenne pepper, nutmeg and paprika. Season to taste with salt and pepper.

3 Toast the sourdough slices under the grill on one side. Spread the cheese mixture on the untoasted sides and cook under a low to medium grill until golden brown and bubbling. Serve immediately.

Will's serving suggestion

Serve with homemade piccalilli, tomato, rocket and shallot salad, mushroom duxelle with fresh truffle, smoked tomato fondue and balsamic jelly or burnt leek puree and onion marmalade.

SHROPSHIRE ONION SOUP

Lesley Mackley - Ludlow

INGREDIENTS

Serves 4

50g butter

1 kg onions, thinly sliced

400 ml Hobsons Twisted Spire

600 ml strong beef stock

Salt and freshly ground black pepper

4 or 8 slices of baguette (depending on size of the loaf)

4 tbsp Oakly Park Cheddar, grated

PREPARATION

1 Place the butter in a large heavy-based pan and heat over a medium heat. When melted and foaming, add the onions and reduce the heat to low. Cook slowly for about 1 hour, stirring occasionally, until the onions are a deep golden brown.

2 Stir in the Hobsons Twisted Spire and the stock and simmer for a further 30 minutes. Season to taste with salt and pepper.

3 Toast the baguette slices under the grill, on one side, then turn them over, cover with the grated cheese and grill until golden and bubbling.

4 Divide the soup between warmed soup bowls and place the cheese toasts on top.

BEEF & BEER TAGINE

Kevin Morrill - Hereford

Kevin Morrill - Hereford

INGREDIENTS

Serves 4-6

650g stewing beef

1 tbsp olive oil

1 large onion, chopped into cubes

2 garlic cloves, crushed

400g can chopped tomatoes

900 ml Hobsons Manor Ale or Best Bitter

1 tsp honey

1 cinnamon stick

400g can chickpeas, drained and rinsed

2 medium courgettes, quartered lengthways
and cut into sticks

2 tbsp chopped fresh coriander

Couscous, to serve

For the spice rub

1 tsp ground cumin

1 tsp ground coriander

2 tsp sweet paprika

PREPARATION

1 To make the spice rub, place all the ingredients in a bowl and mix together. Add the beef and toss well in the spice mixture, to coat thoroughly. Cover and leave overnight in the fridge.

2 Preheat the oven to 180C/Gas 4. Heat the oil in a large casserole. Add the beef, in batches, and brown on all sides. Remove to a plate. Add the onion and garlic (adding a little more oil, if necessary) and cook until soft. Return the beef to the casserole and add the tomatoes, Hobsons Manor Ale or Best Bitter, honey, cinnamon stick and chickpeas. Bring to a simmer, cover and cook in the oven for 1 hour.

3 Reduce the oven temperature to 110C/ Gas ½ and cook for a further 2-3 hours, until the meat is tender and the sauce is thick. Check regularly to make sure the liquid is not drying out. Add more beer, if necessary.

4 Half an hour before the end of the cooking time, add the courgettes. If there appears to be too much liquid, place the uncovered casserole on the hob, on a medium heat, and allow the liquid to reduce. Stir in the coriander and serve with couscous.

Hobsons Best Bitter is only available on draught.

BEEFED UP OLD HENRY BURGER

Mark Williams - Key Cottage Catering, Little Hereford

Old Henry
5.2%
HOBSONS
RICH AUBURN ALE

INGREDIENTS

Makes 8 burgers

1 kg top quality minced beef

2 onions, finely chopped

2 garlic cloves, crushed

125 ml Hobsons Old Henry

2 tbsp fresh white breadcrumbs

2 tbsp Worcester sauce

½ tsp smoked paprika

½ tsp ground cumin

Salt and freshly ground black pepper

Oil for frying

Bread rolls, salad leaves and tomato slices, to serve

PREPARATION

1 In a large bowl, mix together the minced beef, onions, garlic, Hobsons Old Henry, breadcrumbs, Worcester sauce, smoked paprika, cumin, salt and pepper.

2 Divide the mixture into eight and form into burgers, pressing firmly. Heat a little oil in a frying pan and fry the burgers for 4-5 minutes on each side, until browned and cooked through to your liking. Alternatively, brush the burgers with a little oil and grill or barbecue.

3 To serve, place the burgers in rolls with some lettuce and sliced tomatoes.

Variation: For burgers with an oozing, cheesy centre, mould the mixture round a cube of Shropshire Blue cheese.

Note: These quantities are very easily halved to make four burgers.

DRINK THE REST

CHEEKIE PIG & PUY PIE

Henry Mackley - Ludlow Food Centre

Postman's Knock
4.8
HOBSONS
RICH RUBY PORTER
NEWHOUSE FARM
CLEOBURY MORTIMER
Alc 4.8% Vol   500ml

DRINK THE REST

INGREDIENTS

Serves 4

2 tbsp oil

10/12 pigs cheeks

Salt and freshly ground black pepper

300 ml Hobsons Postman's Knock

300 ml veal or chicken stock

150g Puy lentils

100g thick sliced smoked streaky bacon, cut into cubes

1 onion, chopped

1 carrot, chopped

1 celery stick, chopped

2 tbsp chopped fresh parsley

Lemon juice, to taste

1 packet ready-rolled puff pastry

1 egg, beaten, for glazing

PREPARATION

1 Preheat the oven to 140C/Gas 1. Heat half the oil in a heavy-based ovenproof pan with a well-fitting lid. Season the pigs' cheeks and brown in the oil, on both sides. Pour in the Hobsons Postman's Knock and the stock. Bring to a simmer, cover and place in the oven for 3 hours or until the pigs cheeks are very tender. Check from time to time to make sure that the liquid is not drying out and add some more beer and stock, if necessary.

2 Meanwhile, cook the lentils, as directed on the packet, until tender. Drain. Heat the remaining oil in a pan, add the bacon, onion, carrot and celery and cook gently until the bacon is browned and the vegetables are soft. Add the drained lentils to the pan and mix together. Stir in the parsley and lemon juice, to taste. Season with salt and pepper.

3 Preheat the oven to 200C/Gas 6. Place half the lentil mixture in the base of a pie dish. Arrange the cooked pigs cheeks on top and top with the remaining lentils. Pour in enough of the cooking liquid from the meat to thoroughly moisten the lentils.

4 Brush the rim of the pie dish with water. Unroll the pastry and cut narrow strips from one side. Press onto the rim of the dish then brush the pastry rim with water. Place the sheet of pastry over the filling and cut away the excess pastry. Crimp the edge of the pastry with your fingers to make a seal. Make a hole in the middle of the pie. Brush the pastry with beaten egg. Place the pie dish on a baking tray and bake in the oven for about 30 minutes until golden and crisp.

CHICKEN FAJITAS
DO THE TWIST

Holly Searle - Kidderminster

INGREDIENTS

Makes 8

500g skinless chicken breast, cut into strips

1 tbsp oil

1 onion, sliced

1 red pepper, sliced

1 green pepper, sliced

Salt and freshly ground black pepper

Pinch of sugar

2 tbsp chopped fresh coriander

8 tortillas

Salsa and sour cream, to serve

For the marinade

175 ml Hobsons Twisted Spire

Zest and juice of ½ lime

2 garlic cloves, crushed

1 tsp dried oregano

1 tsp ground cumin

1 tsp ground coriander

1 tsp ground cinnamon

½ tsp chilli powder

DRINK
THE
REST

PREPARATION

1. To make the marinade, place all the ingredients in a shallow dish and stir together. Place the chicken strips in the marinade and mix well. Cover and leave to marinate in the fridge for 3 hours.

2. Remove the chicken from the marinade and pat dry with kitchen paper. Heat the oil in a large frying pan and stir fry the chicken until opaque. Add the onions and pepper and continue to stir fry until the vegetables are just soft and the chicken is cooked. Check for seasoning, stir in salt, pepper and a little sugar to taste and add a little more chilli powder, if desired. Add the fresh coriander.

3. Meanwhile, warm the tortillas as directed on the packet. Divide the chicken mixture between the tortillas and roll up tightly. Serve with salsa and sour cream.

DRUNKEN BULLS TAIL

Sandra Jeffries - Fighting Cocks, Stottesdon

INGREDIENTS

Serves 6-8

3 tbsp plain flour

1 tsp ground cinnamon

½ tsp ground nutmeg

Salt and freshly ground black pepper

2 oxtails, cut into pieces and excess fat removed

2 tbsp oil

1 onion, chopped

2 carrots, roughly chopped

1 stick of celery, sliced

2 bottles of Hobsons Twisted Spire

600 ml beef stock

1 cinnamon stick

1 tsp brown sugar

PREPARATION

1 Preheat the oven to 150C/Gas 2. On a plate, mix together the flour, ground cinnamon, nutmeg, salt and pepper. Toss the pieces of oxtail in the flour to coat thoroughly.

2 Heat the oil in a large casserole. Add the oxtail, a few pieces at a time, and brown on all sides. Remove to a plate. Add the onion, carrots and celery and cook until slightly softened, adding a little more oil if necessary.

3 Pour in the Hobsons Twisted Spire and bring gently to the boil, using a wooden spoon to scrape any sediment from the bottom of the casserole. Add the beef stock and return the oxtail to the casserole. Bring gently to a simmer then cover and place in the oven. Cook for 2 ½-3 hours, until the meat starts coming away from the bone. Check from time to time, to make sure the liquid isn't drying out. Add a little more stock or water, if necessary. Turn the pieces of oxtail half way through the cooking time.

4 Remove the oxtail. Strain the sauce through a sieve, pressing the vegetables with a wooden spoon. Skim off any excess fat. Return the sauce to the casserole, stir in the sugar, and, if necessary, boil to reduce slightly. Check the seasoning then replace the oxtail and cinnamon stick and cook for a few minutes until thoroughly heated through. Serve with mashed potatoes and fresh vegetables.

Tip: If possible make this a day ahead, then put the oxtail and sauce in separate bowls and chill overnight. It is then much easier to skim off the fat.

GAZZA'S MILD WILD RABBIT

Gary Seymour - The Sun Inn, Leintwardine

INGREDIENTS

Serves 3-4

2 tbsp plain flour

1 tsp mustard powder

Salt and freshly ground black pepper

1 wild rabbit, jointed

1 tbsp oil

20g butter

4 rashers thick sliced smoked streaky bacon, cut into cubes

2 onions, chopped

2 garlic cloves, crushed

1 bottle Hobsons Postman's Knock

2 tsp Worcester sauce

Sprig fresh rosemary

Sprig fresh thyme

100g button mushrooms

Chopped fresh parsley, to garnish

PREPARATION

1 Preheat the oven to 160C/Gas 3. On a plate, mix together the flour, mustard powder, salt and pepper. Toss the rabbit pieces in the seasoned flour.

2 In a large, heavy-based casserole, heat the oil and butter. Add the rabbit and cook gently until browned all over. Remove from the pan onto a plate. Add the bacon, onion and garlic to the pan and cook until coloured.

3 Stir in the Hobsons Postman's Knock, scraping the bottom of the pan to remove any sediment. Add the Worcester sauce and herbs then return the rabbit to the casserole. Bring to a simmer then cook in the oven for about 2 hours until tender. Check regularly to make sure that the liquid is not drying out. Add some beer or stock, if necessary.

4 Add the mushrooms 30 minutes before the end of the cooking time. Scatter with fresh parsley and serve with herb dumplings.

IN SPIRED
CHICKEN CURRY

John Waring - Orleton

INGREDIENTS

Serves 3-4

4 ripe, but firm, tomatoes

1 tbsp sunflower oil

2 onions, chopped

4 garlic cloves, crushed

2-3 tsp curry powder

300 ml Hobsons Twisted Spire

Salt, to taste

500g skinless, boneless chicken breast or thigh, cut into cubes

½-1 fresh green chilli finely chopped

A squeeze of lemon juice

Chopped coriander, to garnish (optional)

PREPARATION

1 Cut the tomatoes into quarters and remove the seeds. Place in a bowl, cover and microwave on full power for 5 minutes. Leave to cool then remove the 16 pieces of skin

2 In a saucepan, heat the oil. Add the onion and garlic and cook gently for 15 minutes or until soft and golden brown. Add a little water if the onions are browning too quickly. Stir in the curry powder and cook for a minute. Add the Hobsons Twisted Spire and boil rapidly until evaporated.

3 Meanwhile, place the chicken in a microwave dish. Cover and microwave on full power for 3 minutes. Stir, then cover and microwave for a further 2 minutes. Drain the cooking liquid into the pan. Add the tomatoes and chilli and simmer for 15 minutes.

4 At this stage, if a smooth sauce is preferred, whizz in a blender and return to the pan. Otherwise, leave the sauce as it is. Add a little lemon juice, and salt, to taste. Add the chicken and a little water, if required to make the right consistency.

5 Cook gently for a few minutes until the chicken is thoroughly heated through. Scatter with chopped coriander, if using.

Serving suggestions: Serve with rice, a vegetable curry such as sag aloo and side dishes of red onion in yogurt and tarka dhal.

Cook's note: This curry benefits from being prepared the day before eating. Allow to cool then keep, covered, in the fridge overnight. Reheat in the microwave until piping hot.

OLD HENRY'S ORZOTTO

Malcolm Lomax - Buxton

Old Henry

5.2%

HOBSONS
RICH AUBURN ALE

INGREDIENTS

Serves 2-4

1 tbsp olive oil

1 small red onion, finely chopped

150g chestnut mushrooms, sliced

200g pearl barley

150 ml Hobsons Old Henry

1 litre (approximately) hot vegetable stock

Salt and freshly ground black pepper

120g baby spinach leaves

1 small soft goat's cheese

Pumpkin oil, to finish (optional)

PREPARATION

1 Heat the oil in a deep frying pan or shallow casserole. Add the onion and cook for 5 minutes until beginning to soften. Add the mushrooms and cook for a few more minutes, until soft but not coloured. Stir in the pearl barley and cook, stirring, for two more minutes.

2 Add the Hobsons Old Henry and stir until it has evaporated. Keep the vegetable stock hot and gradually add to the barley mixture, stirring constantly, and waiting until it has been absorbed before adding another ladleful.

3 When the barley is just cooked (about 30 minutes), season with salt and pepper then scatter the spinach leaves on top and put a lid on the pan. Leave for a few minutes until the spinach has wilted, then stir into the orzotto. Remove the pan from the heat and crumble in the goat's cheese. Stir in gently. Serve, drizzled with a little pumpkin oil, if desired.

ONE FOOT IN THE GRAVY

Karl Heber Smith - The Church Inn, Ludlow

Old Henry

5.2%

HOBSONS
RICH AUBURN ALE

INGREDIENTS

Serves 4

50 g butter

2 onions, thinly sliced

I garlic clove, crushed

300 ml Hobsons Old Henry

300 ml good beef stock

I tsp grain mustard

Pinch of sugar

Salt and freshly ground black pepper

2 tsp flour

12 good quality thin sausages, cooked

For the mash

750g mashing potatoes eg Maris Piper, peeled and cut into chunks

25g butter

A little milk

DRINK THE REST

PREPARATION

1 In a heavy-based saucepan, melt half the butter. Add the onions and garlic and cook gently, stirring frequently, for 10-15 minutes, until soft and golden brown. Add the Hobsons Old Henry, bring to the boil then simmer until reduced by half. Stir in the stock, bring to the boil then simmer until reduced by half.

2 Meanwhile, cook the potatoes in boiling salted water for 15-20 minutes until quite soft. Drain and mash thoroughly with a potato masher or ricer. Stir in the butter and enough milk to make a smooth mash. Preheat the oven to 190C (Gas 5).

3 Add the mustard to the onion gravy and season to taste with sugar, salt and pepper. In a small bowl, blend together the remaining butter and the flour and whisk into the gravy. Bring to the boil and stir for a few minutes until thickened. Cut each sausage into three pieces and add to the pan. Continue cooking for a few minutes until heated through.

4 Spoon the sausage mixture into a 1.5 litre ovenproof dish. Spoon or pipe the mashed potato on top. Bake in the oven for 20 minutes or until bubbling and golden. Alternatively, place under a grill to brown the top.

TWISTED MUSSELS

Paul Albini - Brewing Director, Hobsons Brewery

INGREDIENTS

Serves 4

1 kg mussels

300 ml Hobsons Twisted Spire

1 large onion, chopped

1 celery stick, chopped

1 carrot, chopped

2 garlic cloves, crushed

6 sage leaves, bruised

20g butter

150g bacon lardons

1 small leek, chopped

150g chestnut mushrooms, chopped

1 tbsp flour

100 ml double cream

450g linguine

PREPARATION

1 Scrub the mussels and remove the beards. Discard any which are broken or do not close when tapped sharply.

2 Place the Hobsons Twisted Spire, 2 garlic cloves (crushed), onion, celery, carrot and sage in a large saucepan and bring to the boil. Add the mussels, cover the pan and continue to boil for 4-6 minutes until the mussels have opened. Discard any which remain closed.

3 Remove the mussels and set aside, leaving the vegetables in the cooking liquid. Boil the liquid until reduced by half then strain through a sieve and reserve. Meanwhile remove the mussels from the shells, keeping a few intact for garnish. Set aside.

4 Heat the butter in a saucepan, add the bacon, leeks and mushrooms and cook until the bacon begins to colour and the vegetables soften. Stir in the flour and cook for a minute. Gradually add the reduced cooking liquid and bring to a simmer then stir in the cream. Add the shelled mussels and heat through.

5 Meanwhile, cook the linguine in boiling, lightly salted water, as directed on the packet. Drain and return to the pan. Stir in the sauce, coating the linguine thoroughly. Serve in warmed bowls, garnished with the reserved mussels in shells.

SAUCY POSTMAN'S PUDDING

Deborah Powell - Cleobury Mortimer

INGREDIENTS

Serves 6-8

200g ready-to-eat-prunes, roughly chopped

250 ml Hobsons Postman's Knock

½ tsp bicarbonate of soda

175g self-raising flour

175g caster sugar

85g butter, softened

2 eggs, beaten

1 tsp vanilla essence

For the Toffee Sauce

284 ml double cream

200g soft brown sugar

200g unsalted butter

3 tbsp Hobsons Postman's Knock

PREPARATION

1 Preheat the oven to 180C/Gas 4. Butter and flour six individual metal pudding basins.

2 Place the prunes and the Hobsons Postman's Knock in a saucepan and bring gently to the boil. Remove from the heat and add the bicarbonate of soda. Mash the prunes with a potato masher to form a pulp. Set aside to cool slightly.

3 Place the flour, sugar, butter, eggs and vanilla essence in a food processor and process until smooth. Alternatively, place all the ingredients in a bowl and beat thoroughly.

4 Add the prune mixture and mix until well combined. Pour the mixture into the prepared pudding basins then place in the centre of the oven and bake for 20-25 minutes until well risen and springy to the touch.

5 Meanwhile, make the toffee sauce. Place the cream, brown sugar, Hobsons Postman's Knock and butter in a saucepan and heat gently until the sugar and butter have melted. Heat until boiling, then simmer for a few minutes, stir until smooth.

6 To serve, turn out the puddings onto individual plates. Pour over some of the sauce and serve the remainder separately.

Variation: This mixture can be baked in a 20 cm square cake tin or oven dish then cut into squares for serving. Allow an extra 5-10 minutes cooking time.

DRINK THE REST

WINNER

Prunes and beer seem an unlikely combination of ingredients, but it works beautifully, producing little sticky puddings with a lovely depth of flavour, and what is more they are very easy to make.

BANANA FRITTERALES

Linda Jones - Mold

INGREDIENTS

Serves 4

75g plain flour

pinch salt

1 ½ tsp caster sugar

1 egg, separated

4 tbsp Hobsons Manor Ale or Best Bitter

25g butter, melted

3 large bananas (not too ripe)

Vegetable oil, for frying

Caster sugar, for dusting

PREPARATION

1   Sift the flour and salt into a bowl and stir in the sugar. Add the egg yolk. Gradually stir in the Hobsons Manor Ale or Best Bitter and then the melted butter. Whisk to make a smooth batter, the consistency of double cream, adding a little water, if necessary. Cover the bowl and leave to stand at room temperature, for about an hour.

2   Just before using, whisk the egg white until it forms soft peaks. Gently fold the egg white into the batter.

3   Heat 5-8 cm oil in a deep frying pan, until it sizzles on contact with a drop of batter. Dip a few pieces of banana in batter then place in the oil. After 2-3 minutes turn the pieces over with a fork. When the fritters are evenly crisp and golden, transfer to kitchen paper to drain. Keep warm while frying the remaining fritters. Dust with caster sugar and serve immediately.

Hobsons Best Bitter is only available on draught.

NOKA CHOC ORANGE RICE CAKE

John Alderman & Nigel Burge - Orleton

Postman's Knock
4.8%
HOBSONS
RICH RUBY PORTER
NEWHOUSE FARM
CLEOBURY MORTIMER
Alc 4.8% Vol.   500ml ℮

INGREDIENTS

Serves 12-16

2 bottles Hobsons Postman's Knock

568 ml milk

200g caster sugar

1 vanilla pod

Grated zest of 1 orange

Grated zest of ½ lemon

300g Arborio rice

100g dark chocolate, roughly chopped

40g raisins

5 large eggs, separated

Zest of 1 orange and icing sugar, to decorate

Orange segments, to serve

PREPARATION

1 Place the Hobsons Postman's Knock, milk, sugar, vanilla pod, orange and lemon zest in a saucepan. Heat gently until the sugar is dissolved then bring to the boil. Stir in the rice and simmer, stirring frequently, on a medium heat for 25-30 minutes until the rice is al dente and has absorbed the liquid, but still has a creamy consistency. Stir chocolate and raisins into rice before allowing it to cool. Set aside to cool. Remove the vanilla pod.

2 Preheat the oven to 180C/Gas 4. Grease and line a 23 cm loose-bottomed cake tin. In a bowl, whisk the egg whites until soft peaks form. In another bowl, whisk the egg yolks until creamy then stir into the cooled rice. Gently fold in the whisked egg whites. Pour into the prepared tin then bake in the oven for about one hour, until golden brown and firm.

3 Leave the cake to cool in the tin for 15 minutes then turn out onto a serving dish, bottom side up. Serve warm or leave to cool completely. To serve, dust with icing sugar and decorate with orange zest. Serve with orange segments.

Tip: For the orange segments, use the oranges which you have zested.

POSTIE'S PURPLE PARCELS

Chrissy Manley - Ludlow

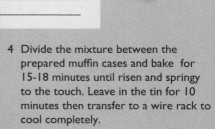

INGREDIENTS

Makes 10

125g unsalted butter

125g 70% dark chocolate

200 ml Hobsons Postman's Knock

1 large egg

125g golden caster sugar

125g cooked beetroot, grated

125g self-raising flour

1 tsp baking powder

Pinch salt

For the frosting

200g butter, softened

150g icing sugar

150g cocoa powder

A 'glug' of Hobsons Postman's Knock

PREPARATION

1 Preheat the oven to 170C/Gas 5. Line 10 holes of a muffin tin with paper muffin cases.

2 Place the butter and chocolate in a bowl set over a pan of simmering water, making sure that the base of the bowl does not touch the water. When melted, remove from the heat.

3 Place the Hobsons Postman's Knock, egg and sugar in a bowl and whisk until frothy then add the chocolate mixture and beat until well combined. Gently squeeze any excess moisture from the beetroot and fold into the chocolate mixture. Sift together the flour, baking powder and salt and fold into the mixture.

4 Divide the mixture between the prepared muffin cases and bake for 15-18 minutes until risen and springy to the touch. Leave in the tin for 10 minutes then transfer to a wire rack to cool completely.

5 To make the frosting, place the butter in a bowl and sift in the icing sugar and cocoa powder. Beat well until smooth, adding a little Hobsons Postman's Knock to make a piping consistency. Either pipe or spread the frosting on top of the cakes.

DRINK THE REST

SPISTED TWIRE SEMIFREDDO

Phil Waring - Cleobury Mortimer Golf Club

Twisted Spire

3/6%

HOBSONS
VIBRANT BLOND BEER

INGREDIENTS

Serves 6-8

2 gelatine leaves

250 ml Hobsons Twisted Spire

150g caster sugar

125 ml water

8 egg yolks

125 ml whipping cream

Crushed peanut brittle, to serve

For the caramel sauce

50g caster sugar

125 ml whipping cream

DRINK
THE
REST

PREPARATION

1. Line a loaf tin, plastic freezer box or terrine dish with clingfilm. Place the gelatine leaves in a shallow dish and cover with water. Leave to soak for about 10 minutes.

2. Heat 60 ml of the Hobsons Twisted Spire in a small saucepan then remove from the heat. Squeeze any excess water out of the gelatine leaves and add to the hot beer. Stir until dissolved then add the remaining beer. Pour into a bowl and leave in the fridge for about one hour until thickened but not set.

3. Place the caster sugar and water in a heavy-based pan and bring to the boil then simmer for 8 minutes. Meanwhile, place the egg yolks in a large bowl and, using an electric whisk, beat until thickened. While whisking, slowly pour in the hot syrup in a steady stream. Keep whisking until the mixture is thick and cool.

4. Place the cream in a bowl and whisk until thickened, but not stiff. Fold the cream into the thickened gelatine mixture then fold this into the egg yolk mixture. Pour into the lined mould, cover and freeze overnight.

5. To make the caramel sauce, warm a heavy-based pan over a medium heat then add the sugar. Still over a medium heat, leave the sugar until it starts to melt and turn to liquid round the edges. (about 5 minutes). Give the pan a shake then leave it until about ¼ of the sugar has melted. Then, with a wooden spoon, stir and continue to cook until the sugar has all melted and the liquid turns a dark golden brown, Carefully stir in the cream (it might splutter) and stir until any lumps of caramel have dissolved and you have a smooth sauce. Allow to cool.

6. To serve the semifreddo, cut slices and place on individual plates. Scatter with roughly crushed peanut brittle, and drizzle over the sauce.

OUR VISION IS TO BECOME THE COUNTRY'S LEADING SUSTAINABLE BREWERY

Sustainability has become an increasingly important part of what we do at Hobsons and over the past couple of years we have strived to reduce our effect on the environment. We know what we do makes sense, we want to do more of it; digest more waste, source more locally, reduce our reliance on statutory providers and become more self sustaining. If this doesn't make us a leader we are not sure what would. Sustainability and responsibility are the only winning way.

Nick Jarvis

Society of Independent Brewers (SIBA) Best Green Business Award 2010 (recognition for our innovative solutions and reduction of carbon emissions.)

SIBA local beer WINNER

We've relished the challenge and embraced leading technologies to achieve our goal of being a sustainable brewery. Here are just a few examples of our super-efficient system …

- We have installed a ground source heat pump to simultaneously heat our bottle conditioning room and cool our barrel store. We were told it wasn't possible but 5 years later . . . proof is in the pudding.

- Four 100m boreholes were drilled providing a constant 11°C of water that is then compressed for heat or cooling or both. It is so efficient that we now keep the girls in the office nice and toasty.

- In 2007 we installed an 11kw GAIA wind turbine. She's a pretty twin blade design that powers about a third of our requirements.

- A rainwater harvesting system was installed to capture surplus rainwater from the extensive roofs of our barrel and bottle store. We utilise this grey water for vehicle washing, general wash-down, hand wash and toilet flushing.

- We have introduced light weight beer bottles that have reduced our packaging waste and made visits to the bottle bank less cumbersome.

Whatever we do, we will always strive for best practice in our brewing and bottling processes and we will continue to be innovative in the ways in which we support our environment.

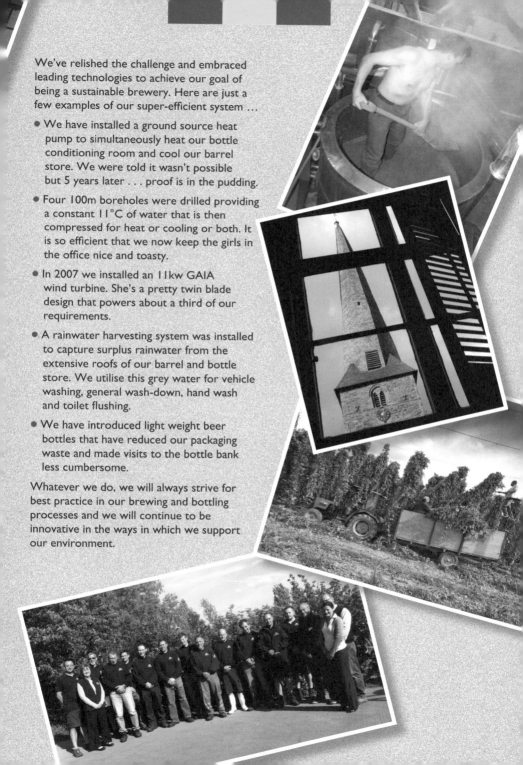

BEER AND FOOD PAIRING

The Hobsons family of beers blend a range of flavours, malt character and hop aromas that compliment a wide variety of foods. Here are a few of our favourite suggestions for beer and food matching that really works. Thank you to our friends Alex Barlow - **www.allbeerfinder.co.uk** and Maggie Wright - **The Deli on the Square** in Ludlow.

Beer	Savoury	Sweet things	Cheeseboard
Mild	Sweet marinated ribs and sausages. Particularly good with all curries	Coffee house cakes such as Florentines, brownies and Black Forest Gateaux	Wensleydale, Cantal, or Bellwether Carmody
Twisted Spire	Lemon chicken or tangy Thai king prawns. Great with seafood, or fish & chips	Lemon tart or Dundee Orange cake	Soft cheeses Wensleydale
Best Bitter	Crusty steak and mushroom pie or pork pie	Sticky Toffee pudding	Double Gloucester or mature Cheddar cheeses
Manor Ale	Cheddar or ham ploughmans, pies or sausages	Homemade bread and butter pudding	Weobley Cheddar Dairylea or Laughing Cow triangles
Town Crier	Roast pork or chicken, leeks and asparagus or stir-fry vegetables	Pavlova	Appleby's Cheshire Double Gloucester cheese
Postman's Knock	BBQ'd red meats, sausages or ribs. Try it with Marmite on toast!	Florentines or rich fruit cake	Mature Cheddar or Shropshire Blue cheese
Old Henry	Roast red meats such as beef, venison or lamb	Fruit cakes, coffee cake or apple & cinnamon tarts	Blue Stilton Berskswell Blue